ALL-NEW! DOUBLE DARE GAME BOOK

by Daniella Burr

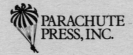

PARACHUTE
PRESS, INC.

For Alison and Alex, two kids who double my fun
all the time!

0-9-38753-27-4
Published by
Parachute Press, Inc.
156 Fifth Avenue
New York, NY 10010

First printing: August 1989
Printed in the U.S.A.
Design by Michel Design

Contents

A DOUBLE DARE contestant slides on through the Obstacle Course.

Can You Answer These Questions?

What TV game show makes its contestants go through challenges called Crossfire Marshmallows and Monster Mashed?

What TV game show quizzes kids on subjects ranging from world travels to Bon Jovi?

What TV game show has gakky obstacle courses with stations called the Sundae Slide and the Hamster Wheel?

What TV game show is the super-sloppiest, wild and wackiest show of them all?

If you answered DOUBLE DARE™ to all the questions above, you are our kind of kid—a DOUBLE DARE fan! And the ALL-NEW DOUBLE DARE Game Book is just your kind of book!

The ALL-NEW DOUBLE DARE Game Book is filled with official DOUBLE DARE questions and fun and frantic DOUBLE DARE physical challenges. Some are sloppy and some are not—so you can have DOUBLE DARE fun inside and out! There are even two official DOUBLE DARE obstacle courses you can set up to try at home!

1

But that's not all! The ALL-NEW DOUBLE DARE Game Book gives you the inside scoop on the goop behind the scenes, with lots of DOUBLE DARE fast facts. There's even a chapter to show you how to have a dynamite DOUBLE DARE overnight!

The first part of the book is set up just like the game on TV. Play it yourself and see how many points you can rack up. Or play against another DOUBLE DARE kid. You might want to get a gang of DOUBLE DARE fans together and play in teams—just like on TV!

Whatever you decide, you'll have hours of DOUBLE DARE fun with the ALL-NEW DOUBLE DARE Game Book. It's got everything the TV show has—except maybe Mark and Harvey!

Chapter One

Here Come the Questions!!

What color is an orange?

What fruit is in an apple pie?

Who is buried in Grant's tomb?

Okay, the questions in this chapter are a little bit tougher than those three. But you are sharp enough to tackle even the toughest questions.

And that's important, because this chapter is full of questions. Some are tough and some are easy, but they all come from the DOUBLE DARE TV show!

Each page has four questions on it. The first two are DARE questions. They are worth 20 points each. If you are feeling extra-daring, skip the DARE questions and try the DOUBLE DARE questions for double the points. The answers are upside down at the bottom of each page.

If the questions aren't your style, you can try the physical challenge. Just follow the instructions on the bottom of each page. They'll lead you where you need to go to get in a real mess (of fun that is!). Since most of the physical challenges have time limits, keep a stopwatch or a watch with a second hand nearby. A pad and a pencil will help you keep the score straight.

When you finish a physical challenge, check the instructions at the bottom of the page. They'll tell you how to score the challenge, and they'll put you back on the right question track.

Any questions? Good! Now let's get to it!

Being the host of DOUBLE DARE can be a
dirty job—but Marc Summers can face
anything!

5

Ha ha ha! These comic questions will tickle your funny bone!

DARE
1. Which Peanuts character is always messing up Charlie Brown's big chance to kick a football?
2. In the Archie comic-book series, Jughead Jones has a fluffy white dog. Name the crazy canine.

DOUBLE DARE
1. What comic-strip character did Cathy Guisewhite create?
2. In an alphabetical list, which of Donald Duck's nephews is last?

If these questions had you stumped, why not have the last laugh and try the funny physical challenge on page 27?

If these questions had you stumped, why not have the last laugh and try the funny physical challenge on page 27?

Answers:
DARE: 1. Lucy
2. Hot Dog

DOUBLE DARE: 1. Cathy
2. Louie (Dewey, Huey, Louie)

You seem like a worldly kind of kid! You certainly won't have any trouble answering these tough travel questions.

DARE
1. Name the Queen of England
2. In what state can you visit a statue of Tony the Tiger and see the Kellogg's factory?

DOUBLE DARE
1. If you wore a *lei* at a *luau*, what state would you be probably dining in?
2. Budapest is the capital of what country?

If all that traveling left your brain with jet lag, or if you are just the adventurous type who likes a challenge (the physical kind), turn to page 28.

~~~~~~

Answers:
DARE: 1. Queen Elizabeth II
2. Michigan (Battle Creek)

DOUBLE DARE: 1. Hawaii
2. Hungary (no . . . I just ate dinner!
Ha ha—just a quick DOUBLE DARE joke break!)

DOUBLE DARE kids know what's what. So what are the answers to the questions?

DARE
1. What classical stringed instrument is bigger than a violin or viola but smaller than a bass fiddle?
2. What amusement-park ride did George Ferris invent?

DOUBLE DARE
1. Flattop, beehive, and Mohawks are all types of what?
2. What common gas is pumped into soda pop to make it bubbly?

What's more fun than a DOUBLE DARE physical challenge—nothing! So why not try the challenge that's waiting for you on page 29?

~~~~~~~~~~~~~~~~~~~~~~~~~~~~~~~~~~

Answers:
DARE: 1. Cello
2. The Ferris wheel
DOUBLE DARE: 1. Hairdos
2. Carbon dioxide

8

You'll get these right without a shadow of a doubt!

DARE
1. When you are shadow-boxing, who are you fighting against?
2. In what story does a girl named Wendy sew a shadow on a boy who lost it?

DOUBLE DARE
1. What does it mean to have a five-o'clock shadow?
2. When is your shadow longest?
  A. Morning
  B. Afternoon
  C. Evening

If these shadow questions have you in the dark, why don't you head over to page 30 and try the physical challenge?

Answers:
DARE: 1. An imaginary opponent or yourself
2. *Peter Pan*
DOUBLE DARE: 1. You need a shave
2. B. Afternoon

9

These DOUBLE DARE questions were designed with your mind in mind!

DARE

1. On a popular TV sitcom, what is Charlie Moore's job?
2. How many all-beef patties are in a McDonald's Big Mac?

DOUBLE DARE
1. In *The Hobbit*, what is the name of the wizard who befriends and guides Bilbo Baggins?
2. What Michael Jackson video takes place in a subway station?

Are you experiencing brain drain? Then why not let your body take over with the physical challenge on page 31?

Sometimes the questions can get pretty heavy!
But you can carry them off!

DARE
1. Where on your body would you wear a goatee?
2. In *Alice in Wonderland*, what lawn game does
Alice play with the Queen of Hearts?

DOUBLE DARE
1. What sport did Ty Cobb, Peewee Reese, and
Hank Aaron play?
2. A groundhog is also known as what mammal?

Is your head feeling heavy under all this
pressure? Then take a load off and go to page 32
for something physical!

Answers:
DARE: 1. On your face, it's a beard.
2. Croquet
DOUBLE DARE: 1. Baseball
2. Woodchuck

Paging all bookworms—these questions are for you.

DARE
1. In what town did Dr. Seuss's Cindy Lou Who live?
2. How did Pippi Longstocking wear her hair?

DOUBLE DARE
1. In one of Shakespeare's greatest plays, a character calls from the balcony, "Romeo, Romeo, wherefore art thou, Romeo?" Name her.
2. In the Dr. Doolittle stories, what type of animal is Dab Dab?

All booked up? Turn over a new leaf on page 33 with a brand-new physical challenge!

Answers:
DARE: **1.** Whoville (from *How the Grinch Stole Christmas*)
2. In pigtails
DOUBLE DARE: **1.** Juliet
2. A duck

It's time to go through the DOUBLE DARE time machine and try these history questions.

DARE
1. Who was president of the United States just before George Bush?
2. During the U.S. Civil War, which side called itself the Union—the North or the South?

DOUBLE DARE
1. Ivan the Terrible and Peter the Great were both leaders of what country?
2. Who was the first American astronaut to orbit the earth in a spaceship?

If a trip down memory lane isn't your idea of excitement, blast over to page 34 for an historic physical challenge.

Answers:
DARE: 1. Ronald Reagan
2. The North
DOUBLE DARE: 1. The Soviet Union
2. John Glenn

Channel your energies toward answering these TV trivia questions.

DARE
1. According to the *Brady Bunch* theme song, how did the youngest girl wear her hair?
2. On *Star Trek: The Next Generation*, what is the name of the spaceship?

DOUBLE DARE
1. On the old TV show *Family Affair* what was the name of the family butler and nanny?
    A. Mr. French
    B. Mr. Magoo
    C. Mr. Mister
2. Shaggy, Velma, and Daphne are all friends of what cartoon dog?

If you've had enough of these TV questions, change the station and turn to the physical challenge on page 35.

Answers:
DARE: 1. In curls
2. *The Enterprise*
DOUBLE DARE: 1. A. Mr. French
2. Scooby Doo

Come on, be a pal. Try one of these fun friendship questions.

DARE
1. Who was Lucy's best friend on *I Love Lucy*?
2. What comic strip stars a young boy and his best friend, a stuffed tiger?

DOUBLE DARE
1. Who was Tom Sawyer's best friend?
2. What is the name of Porky Pig's girlfriend?

Have all these quizzes made you a bit testy? Try a challenge on page 36 instead!

DOUBLE DARE Fast Fact: Every single physical challenge on DOUBLE DARE has a name. Even if you don't hear the name on the show, the writers have given the challenge a funny name. Sometimes the writers think of the name first, and then think up a challenge to go with it.

Answers:
DARE: 1. Ethel (Mertz)
2. Calvin and Hobbes
DOUBLE DARE: 1. Huckleberry Finn
2. Petunia

Time for a DOUBLE DARE poetry break...
    DOUBLE DARE asks the questions,
    You may think they're a strain,
    But think of them in this way:
    As push-ups for the brain!

DARE

1. The White House is located on an avenue with what state's name?

2. What kind of fruit is in Fig Newtons?

DOUBLE DARE

1. How many rings are in the Olympic circle?

2. According to the *Official Boy Scout Handbook*, which of the following is not a specific merit badge?

    A. Ant farming
    B. Dentistry
    C. Dog care

Are these quizzes driving you quazy? Then try the physical challenge on page 38 (and go totally nuts).

Answers:
DARE: 1. Pennsylvania (1600 Pennsylvania Avenue)
2. Figs
DOUBLE DARE: 1. Five
2. A. Ant farming

Here's a mixed bag of DOUBLE DARE questions.

DARE
1. On what part of your body would you wear a turban?
2. What two countries border Lake Huron?

DOUBLE DARE
1. What was President Hoover's first name?
2. *Packard* and *Edsel* are types of what?

Feeling brave? Why not try the challenge that's waiting for you on page 39?

  DOUBLE DARE Fast Fact: The chocolate gak on the sundae slide is actually chocolate pudding.

Answers:
DARE: 1. On your head, it's a hat
2. Canada and the United States
DOUBLE DARE: 1. Herbert
2. Cars

17

Rack up big numbers of points with these number questions.

DARE
1. How many stars are on the U.S. flag?
2. What number would you get if you added the number of dwarfs in *Snow White* with the number of sides that a triangle has?

DOUBLE DARE
1. If the kids from *Kate and Allie, Mr. Belvedere*, and *Growing Pains* got together, how many boys would there be?
2. What number do you get if you add together the number of years Sleeping Beauty slept and the number of days in a leap year?

If you were counting on a physical challenge, take a look at page 40.

Wait! Your number isn't up yet. Here are four more number questions.

DARE
1. How many official languages does Canada have?

2. Musically speaking, how many quarter notes equal a whole note?

DOUBLE DARE
1. How many members are there in the serial number of a dollar bill?

2. In Roman numerals, V + V equals what Roman numeral?

Tired of numbers? Subtract yourself from this page and try the physical challenge on page 41.

These food questions are all in very good taste!

DARE
1. Wisconsin, the Dairy State, once made it illegal to sell what?
   A. Parmesan cheese
   B. Margarine
   C. Elsie the Cow statues
2. If you soaked a slice of bread in eggs and milk and then fried it, what would you be making for breakfast?

DOUBLE DARE
1. If you ordered a pie à la mode, what would be on top of the pie?
2. The dachsund sausage was another name for what popular food?

If nothing on the question menu tingles your tastebuds, why not try a DOUBLE DARE physical challenge on page 42?

why not try a DOUBLE DARE physical challenge on page 42?

Answers:
DARE: 1. B. Margarine
2. French toast
DOUBLE DARE: 1. Ice cream
2. The hot dog

These questions are as tough as a week-old hot dog. But you're sharp enough to cut the mustard!

DARE
1. A ram is a male what?
2. Of mice and rats, which have hairless tails?

DOUBLE DARE
1. How long is a U.S. president's term of office?
2. Actor River Phoenix has brothers and sisters with equally interesting first names. Name any two of them.

Are you stumped? Then turn to page 43 for your personalized physical challenge.

Are you stumped? Then turn to page 43 for your personalized physical challenge.

wwwwwwwwwwwwwwwwwwwwww

DOUBLE DARE Fast Fact: Did you know that every physical challenge and every obstacle on DOUBLE DARE is tested by kids before it's ever tried on the air?

wwwwwwwwwwwwwwwwwwwwww

2. Leaf, Rainbow, Liberty, Summer
DOUBLE DARE: 1. Four years

2. Rats
DARE: 1. Sheep
Answers:

Treat these questions like a cold swimming pool on a hot summer's day. Dive right in!

DARE
1. At the Olympics, what score would a judge give you for a perfect gymnastics performance?
2. What chess piece can move in the most directions?

DOUBLE DARE
1. According to the folk song, where do the deer and the antelope play?
2. What is a soothsayer?
    A. Someone who says "sooth" a lot
    B. A person who predicts the future
    C. A member of the British Parliament

If you can't answer your question, swim on over to page 44 for a physical challenge.

Answers:
DARE: 1. 10
2. The queen
DOUBLE DARE: 1. On the range
2. A person who predicts the future

22

It's time for the DOUBLE DARE name game. How good are you at naming names?

DARE
1. In the movies, what giant ape had a "royal" name?
2. Name the Popeye character that will "gladly pay you Tuesday" for a hamburger.

DOUBLE DARE
1. Name the first bearded president of the United States.
2. In Mary Shelley's book *Frankenstein*, what character creates the monster?

If you are game for a physical challenge, turn to page 45.

Answers:
DARE: 1. King Kong
2. Wimpy
DOUBLE DARE: 1. Abraham Lincoln
2. Dr. Frankenstein

Stop your quest. Here are the questions you've been searching for!

DARE

1. Is a *calliope* a melon, a musical instrument, or a cape?

2. What suspect in the game of *Clue* has the same name as a fruit?

DOUBLE DARE

1. What do Mark Twain, Thomas Edison, and Charles Dickens all have in common?

    A. They all tried for Harvey's job

    B. They never graduated from high school

    C. They were all famous inventors

2. Comets, nymphs, and fantails are varieties of what kind of popular pet fish?

If you are still searching for something to do, try the challenge on page 47.

If you are still searching for something to do, try the challenge on page 47.

Answers:
DARE: 1. A musical instrument
2. Professor Plum

DOUBLE DARE: 1. B. They never graduated from high school
2. Goldfish

Chapter Two

Let's Get Physical

Double-daring displays of dynamite deeds!

That's the definition of DOUBLE DARE's physical challenges. Your first challenge is to twist your tongue by saying *that* three times fast. When you're through, you can wind down by reading this page.

This chapter is filled with physical challenges. You don't need a lot of supplies to do the challenges, all you need is a little skill and a lot of nerve. Most of the challenges are designed to be played with a partner, but if you are playing alone, there are special instructions on how to take on the challenge alone.

Score 40 points for each challenge you do successfully. Then read the instructions on the bottom of each page. They'll set you back on track for your next set of questions.

Good luck!

A DOUBLE DARE contestant gets the point of this physical challenge. It's called Velcro Darts.

Jumping Jellybeans!

Whoever thought those little pieces of sugar could be such a handful!

You will need:

    4 mittens
    10 jellybeans
    1 Styrofoam cup

Time limit: 20 seconds

The play: Spread the jellybeans all over the floor. Put the cup in the middle of the floor. All you and your partner have to do is collect all 10 jellybeans and put them in the cup. Oh, yeah . . . one more thing . . . You have to wear the mittens while you're picking up the beans. But that's the little secret—now, don't spill the beans, okay?

Challenge for one: If you're trying this one by yourself, sweeten the treat by giving yourself five extra seconds.

If you've gotten all the beans in on time, add 40 points to your score and jump on over to page 7 for some quizzing questions!

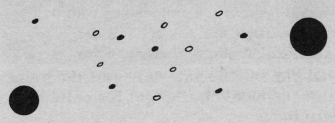

Rock and Roll Romp!

Finish this musical challenge and you'll note a nice change in your score!

You will need:
10 music cassettes and their cases

Time limit: 20 seconds

The play: The cassettes and cases are separated and spread out all over the floor. It's up to the two of you to sort through the musical mess and get five cassettes back in their right cases before the time is up.

Challenge for one: If you are trying this as a solo artist add 5 seconds to your time limit.

If you pass the challenge, give yourself a reward to the tune of 40 points. Then let's pick up the tempo and hurry over to page 8.

DOUBLE DARE Fast Fact: What's the difference between DOUBLE DARE and the new SUPER-SLOPPY DOUBLE DARE? About 200 gallons—of whipped cream. DOUBLE DARE used 200 gallons of whipped cream a day. SUPER-SLOPPY DOUBLE DARE uses 400 gallons a day.

Ready . . . Set . . . Drop!

You really have to be on the ball to beat this challenge!

You will need:
   1 basketball
   1 blindfold

Time limit: 15 seconds

The play: You stand on one side of the room with your legs spread apart. Your partner rolls the basketball to you. You have to stop the rolling ball by sitting on it while it is still in motion. You only have to do it once, but it is harder than you think, because you'll be wearing a blindfold. That means it's up to the roller to yell "Now!" when it's time to sit.

Challenge for one: If you are trying this on your own, you have to roll the ball, then run to the other side of the room and sit on the basketball before it crosses the line. It sounds pretty tough, but you get the added advantage of not having to wear the blindfold.

When you're through having a ball with this challenge, give yourself 40 points and roll on over to page 9 for a new question.

Map Happy

Your future is all mapped out for you with this challenge.

You will need:
   1 road map

Time limit: 40 seconds

The play: Before you begin, unfold the road map. Now all you have to do is fold it up again. Once it is all neatly folded into its proper original shape, unfold it and pass it to your partner. Your partner then has to fold it again.

Challenge for one: You only have to fold it once—so your time limit is 20 seconds.

If you went the distance in the time allotted, add 40 points to your score and drive back to page 10 for a new question.

〰〰〰〰〰〰〰〰〰〰〰〰〰〰

DOUBLE DARE Fast Fact: The kids on DOUBLE DARE always choose their own partners. They try out for the show as a team. In fact, teamwork is the most important part of doing well at DOUBLE DARE. If a team communicates well, they do well.

〰〰〰〰〰〰〰〰〰〰〰〰〰〰

The DOUBLE DARE Tea Party

This challenge will fit you to a tea!

You will need:
    5 tea bags (ask your parents for permission first)
    1 paper or plastic cup

Time limit: 25 seconds

The play: All you have to do is stand two feet from your partner and toss a tea bag into the cup your partner is holding. However, to put some bite into this challenge you must use your teeth for the toss. So bite on the string, give the bag a swing, and let it go!

Challenge for one: Put the mug on a table two feet away from you. Since the table has legs but no arms, it can't move to catch your tea bag. So, give yourself an additional 10 seconds.

Once you've got this tea challenge in the bag, add 40 points to your score and turn to page 11 for a new question.

Test Pilot!

You have to get the challenge off the ground if you want the points!

You will need:
  10 square sheets of paper
  A finish line set up 10 feet from start (a belt lying on the floor makes a good finish line)

Time limit: 15 seconds

The play: All you and your partner have to do is make one paper airplane and send it on a 10-foot flight across the room, past the finish line.

Challenge for one: Since you're going to be flying solo, add 5 seconds to your expected arrival time.

Once you've come in for your landing, add 40 points to your score and fly on to page 12 for the questions.

Miracle Cure

Can the DOUBLE DARE players save the patient?

You will need:
  1 inflated balloon
  1 bath towel
  1 bucket

Time limit: 20 seconds

The play: The balloon is the injured victim, and you and your partner are the emrgency rescue squad. Each of you must take one end of a towel and stretch it tight like a stretcher. Place the balloon on the towel. Now hurry the patient across the room and to the hospital (right, get the balloon in the bucket). Remember, any time your patient (balloon) hits the ground, you have to pick it up and start all over. And once the patient is on your stretcher, you can't touch him. You must use the towel to drop the balloon in the bucket.

Challenge for one: Since you'll be holding the towel alone, try a smaller face towel. Holding each end with one hand, give yourself an extra five seconds.

Once the patient is in the care of the hospital doctors, treat yourself to another question on page 13.

Marshmallow Rally

You will need:
> 2 tennis rackets, Ping-Pong paddles, or 2
> plastic plates will work
> 3 marshmallows
> 1 wastebasket

Time limit: 20 seconds

The play: Welcome to the exciting world of
DOUBLE DARE tennis. You and your partner each
get a racket. All you have to do is walk down the
court to the basket, hitting a marshmallow back
and forth between you. You must get all three
marshmallows in the basket to get the points.

Challenge for one: If you are playing your own
game of tennis, use only one racket, bounce the
marshmallow up and down on your racket. Give
yourself five extra seconds to do it.

If you got all three marshmallows in the basket,
you've just netted an extra 40 points! Now go to
page 14 for a new set of questions.

Balloon Doom

Try a little balloon-acy!

You will need:
>   8 blown-up balloons
>   1 blindfold

Time limit: 15 seconds

The play: The balloons are set up in a big pile. You wear the blindfold. Feel your way around and pick up one balloon at a time. Hand the balloon to your partner. Your partner must hold on to that balloon as you hand him or her the next one. If your partner drops any balloons, you must start over. Once your partner has six balloons, you can stop.

Challenge for one: Put on the blindfold and grab the balloons yourself. But hold on tight— we're only making you pile up four of them.

Did you make it? Then add 40 points and float over to page 15.

Feeding Time!

Even wild animals need to eat sometime!

You will need:
    5 marshmallows
    1 blindfold

Time limit: 15 seconds

The play: Your partner throws the marshmallows at you. You have to catch them in your mouth. But we've sweetened the challenge by making your partner wear a blindfold while he or she is throwing. Catch two marshmallows and the points are yours.

Challenge for one: Forget the blindfold, but keep one hand behind your back. Toss the marshmallows up and catch them in your own mouth. Oh, and fair is fair—since you can see the marshmallows, you only get 10 seconds.

If you've finished your meal, give yourself 40 sweet points. Then go to page 16 for a new and exciting challenge!

Hey, they don't call it gak for nothing!

Heads Up!

You'll have to use your heads if you want to get the points!

You will need:
    1 balloon

Time limit: 15 seconds

The play: Both players put their hands behind their backs. Now, using your heads only, keep the balloon in the air while you walk it across the room. If the balloon drops before you reach the other side of the room, go back and start again.

Challenge for one: Since going head to head is impossible when you have only one head, you must bounce the balloon off your head to keep it in the air. Give yourself an extra 10 points for the extra effort.

If you've succeeded in this challenge, you can hold your heads high! Give yourself 40 points and head back to page 17. There you can use your head to answer a new question.

Having a Ball!

The points will come rolling in!

You will need:
Soccer ball, basketball, or any other large ball

Time limit: 15 seconds

The play: Instead of kicking the soccer ball, you have to place it between your knees and walk across the room, keeping the ball in place. If you drop the ball, you must go back. Once you and your partner have each had a trip across the room, tally up the points and roll on.

Challenge for one: Since you must walk both ways, give yourself five extra seconds.

Did you get a kick out of this one? Then bounce over to page 18 for a question.

Pass That Ball!

You will need:

   large cotton balls
   2 straws
   1 bowl
   2 chairs
   1 table

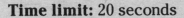

Time limit: 20 seconds

The play: You both sit at the table with straws in your mouths. All you have to do is pick up a cotton ball by sucking in your straw. Then pass the ball to your partner's straw without letting it drop. Your partner can then let the cotton ball drop into the bowl. Three cotton balls into the bowl and the points are yours!

Challenge for one: Put the bowl on the opposite side of the table. Then pick up the cotton ball, get up, and walk over to the bowl and let it drop. Three in and you get 40 points.

Once the passes are completed, give yourself 40 points and pass on over to page 19 for a quick question.

Tricky Turn

It's your turn to do something really difficult!

You will need:
  1 pair of sweat socks
  1 magazine

Time limit: 20 seconds

The play: This is a challenge for one. Decide who is going to try it—you or your partner. Now, all you have to do is read a magazine. There is one small catch; you have to wear the sweat socks—on your hands! If you can turn five pages of the magazine with the socks on, you get a socko 40 points!

If you've earned the points, it's time to turn to page 20.

DOUBLE DARE Fast Fact: Yes, Marc, Harvey, and the producers of DOUBLE DARE have all run through the obstacle course. According to producer, Mike Klinghoffer, the Gumball Machine is the most fun.

Nose Hockey

You've got to win this one by a nose!

You will need:
   1 checkerboard
   1 red checker
   1 black checker

Time limit: 20 seconds

The play: Put the checkerboard on the floor with the red checker at one end, and the black checker at the other. Now you and your partner kneel down on the floor on opposite sides of the board. All you have to do is push your checker to the opposite side of the board with your nose. Of course, while you're going one way, your partner is coming at you from the other side. And if your checker goes off the board, you have to start all over again.

Challenge for one: The rules are the same, get your checker across. But you have to do it in 15 seconds.

All done? Add 40 points to your score and check out the questions on page 21.

It's in the Bag!

If laundry is your bag, you'll clean up in this challenge!

You will need:

- 1 laundry bag
- 1 pair of jeans
- 1 T-shirt
- 1 pair of socks

Time limit: 20 seconds

The play: All you have to do is toss the clothing into the laundry bag your partner is holding five feet from you.

Challenge for one: Instead of a laundry bag, use a laundry basket. Rest the basket on the floor five feet from you. We'll even throw in five extra seconds!

Did you do it? Then give yourself 40 points and spin over to page 22 for a question.

Traffic Jam

It's bumper to bumper on the DOUBLE DARE Freeway!

You will need:
    6 plastic cups
    1 five-foot piece of string
    1 blindfold

Time limit: 30 seconds

The play: Set the cups up in a straight line with three feet between each cup. One partner should be the driver and the other one the car. The car ties the string around his or her waist. The car also puts on the blindfold. It's up to the driver to lead the car around each cup all the way to the other side of the room—without knocking over any cups. Knock one over and you have to start all over again!

Challenge for one: You get to be the driver and the car. So, make like a small sports car by getting down on all fours. Now you have to crawl between the cups. You don't have to wear the blindfold. It's not as easy as it sounds—sometimes it's tough to control the tail end!

When you are through, get off at the nearest exit, add 40 points to your score, and drive over to page 23.

What a Turnoff!

You will need:
portable alarm clock
portable radio
portable cassette player with a cassette in it
(or you can use a kitchen timer, a battery-
operated toy with on/off switch, a portable
vacuum, etc.)

Time limit: 20 seconds

The play: Put the clock, the radio, and the
cassette player on a table. Use portable ones, so
there are no plugs to pull out. Turn them all on at
once, including the alarm. Now you and your
partner put on the blindfolds. You have 20
seconds to work together and turn everything off!

Challenge for one: Since you are going this
alone, the timer's giving you an extra five
seconds!

If everything is turned off, give yourself 40 points
and turn on to page 24 for a new question.

DOUBLE DARE Fast Fact: When they made the very first DOUBLE DARE show, they had to stop and start the obstacle course four times. Why? On the very first obstacle, the kids were supposed to find the flag inside a big feather pillow. So they started again —but they still couldn't find the flag. It wasn't there this time, either. It seems Marc thought the producer had put the flag in the obstacle, and the producer thought Marc had done it. So they started a third time. This time the kids found the flag, but a cameraman got in the way, and the kids ran right into him. So they had to start for the fourth time! This time the kids went all the way through!

And the Fans Love It!

Here's a fan-tastic challenge to try.

You will need:
> 2 paper fans (if you don't have any fans, you can make them out of plain paper)
> 1 Ping-Pong ball
> 1 paper cup
> 1 table

Time limit: 20 seconds

The play: Put the paper cup on its side and tape it to the end of the table. Put the Ping-Pong ball on the other end of the table. Now use the fans to blow the ball across the table. You cannot touch the ball with the fans. You and your partner are going to have to work together to guide the ball in the right direction. Get the ball in the cup and you win the points.

Challenge for one: The rules are the same, but since you're playing solo, give yourself an extra 10 seconds.

Did you reach your goal? Then give yourself 40 points and add up your score. This is the last challenge of this round.

An Obstacle Course runner goes through the Snowstorm.

Chapter Three

Extra-Gakky Physical Challenges

When you're playing DOUBLE DARE, "gak" is where it's at. But remember—only try the extra-gakky stuff outside. Wear old clothes. *And* always get a parent's permission. Otherwise, you could wind up in a *real* mess (of trouble).

If you are keeping score, give yourself 40 points for each extra-gakky physical challenge you complete. You can do one of these sloppy physical challenges instead of any of the physical challenges in the last chapter.

Come Clean

You will need:
> 1 watering can
> a tub of water for refilling the can if necessary
> soap
> 1 blindfold

Time limit: 20 seconds

The play: Before you begin, get your hands completely soaped up. Then your partner, wearing the blindfold, of course, has to fill up the watering can, walk over to you, and spill the water on your hands. You can't touch or speak to your partner as he or she tries to clean you up.

DOUBLE DARE Fast Fact: Some obstacles are designed but never make it to the show. For example, they tried to do an obstacle called Barber Chair. The idea was, you'd pump yourself up in the chair until you were high enough to reach the flag. The only problem was they couldn't figure out how you'd get down!

Beat It!

This challenge is overflowing with fun.

You will need:
    1 large mixing bowl
    1 old-fashioned eggbeater or wire whisk
    dishwasher detergent
    water

Time limit: 30 seconds

The play: Before you begin, put enough water in the bowl to come two-thirds of the way to the top. Add two drops of detergent. Now all you have to do is beat it. Use the wire whisk or the beater and keep at it until the bubbles flow over the top of the bowl. If you are playing with a partner, take turns.

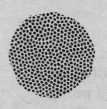

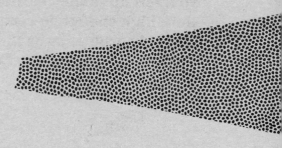

Wild, Wet, and Wacky!

You'll love this watered-down challenge!

You will need:
    6 sponges
    1 bucket of water
    1 empty bucket

Time limit: 15 seconds

The play: All you have to do is hold the empty bucket and catch the sponges your partner throws at you. Pretty simple—right? Of course, you do have to hold the bucket on your head to catch them. Stand with your back to your partner with the bucket on your head. One more thing— the sponges have been soaking in the bucket of water. Hey, these things are called challenges, aren't they? Catch four and you'll soak up 40 points.

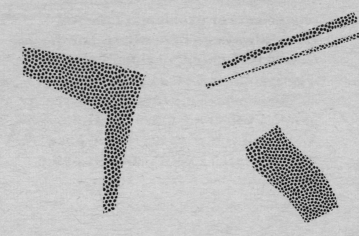

Planet of the Grapes

This challenge is di-vine!

You will need:
  20 grapes (get permission from your parents
  first)
  2 basketballs

Time limit: 15 seconds

The play: The grapes are spread around on the
ground, outside, please! You and your partner
must stand three feet away from the grapes. It
is up to you and your partner to bounce the
basketball and squish six grapes. Take turns.
Here's hoping you have grape aim!

**DOUBLE DARE Fast Fact: There are
some secrets to doing well on the
obstacles. For example, in the Ant
Farm, always go in feetfirst. For the
Gumball Machine, decide in advance
where your partner is going to stand,
so you can have the flag in the correct
hand as you come down the slide.
And when you're going up the nose,
always search in both nostrils at the
same time.**

Broom Around the Room

You need to make a clean sweep of this one to get the points.

You will need:
> Confetti or small pieces of ripped-up paper
> 1 broom
> 1 dustpan
> 1 blindfold
> 1 trash can

Time limit: 20 seconds

The play: The confetti is spread out all over the ground. You hold the dustpan while your blindfolded partner sweeps the confetti into it. Then you have to dump the confetti into the trash can. Clean it all up before time is up, and the points are yours.

DOUBLE DARE Fast Fact: One time, the DOUBLE DARE tank was filled with vanilla pudding. Disgusting? When you jumped in, the pudding was so thick, you couldn't move.

Inside Scoop

Beat this corny challenge and you'll be very popular!

You will need:
   3 large bags of popcorn
   2 empty one-pound butter or margarine tubs
   3 Styrofoam cups
   1 large trash bag

Time limit: 20 seconds

The play: Before you start, pour the popcorn into the trash bag. All you have to do is use the tubs to scoop out the corn. Then run across the room and pour the popcorn into the Styrofoam cups. You can't use your hands to keep the cups still, and you must pour the popcorn directly from the tubs to the cups. (No helping with your hands.) Fill all three cups and the points are yours.

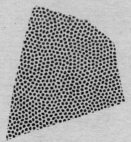

That Something Eggs-tra!

Here's a chance to be the Easter Bunny.

You will need:
    1 egg
    2 felt-tipped pens

Time limit: 30 seconds

The play: Handle this one with care. Take a raw egg and carefully write your name on it. Then hop on one foot to your partner, who is standing five feet away from you. Your partner has to autograph the egg, too, and then hop back to you. Keep signing and hopping until the entire shell is covered in writing. Do it in 30 seconds without breaking the egg and you win 40 points.

I Love Juicy

Put your best foot forward for this wild, wet challenge!

You will need:
   5 water balloons
   1 bucket

Time limit: 30 seconds

The play: Remember—do this outside—it's a wet one! Put a water balloon in the bucket. Then step on it until the water oozes out like juice from a grape. Then give your partner a chance. Keep taking turns until all the balloons have been popped.

DOUBLE DARE Fast Fact: DOUBLE DARE used to be taped in Philadelphia, but now it is made in Orlando, Florida. The biggest difference, according to Mike Klinghoffer, is the weather. "We used to have to get down and scrub and clean everything on DOUBLE DARE. Now we just take it outside and hose it off!"

Marc helps a contestant go through "In the Ear".

Chapter Four

All right!
It's a
DOUBLE DARE
Overnight!

Who says your DOUBLE DARE fun has to stop at sunset? You and your pals can keep the DOUBLE DARE action going all night long when you get together for a DOUBLE DARE overnight!

Slithering Snakes!

We know you are going to play DOUBLE DARE at your overnight (that is why you got together, isn't it?), but here's another silly game that will get your guests in the mood for those DOUBLE DARE physical challenges.

You will need:
2 handkerchiefs
a room with lots of open space

The play: Have your friends get in two lines, with the same number of people in each line. Each guest holds on to the next person in line by putting his or her arms around the waist of the person in front of him or her. The last person in line has a handkerchief tucked in his or her belt loop. The object of the game is for the first person in line to grab the handkerchief from the last person in the other line. But no one in either line can let go of the person in front of him or her. So you have to twist around like a slithering snake, trying to get the front of your line near the back of the other line without getting your back too close to their front. You've got to try it—it's ssssoooo sssilly!

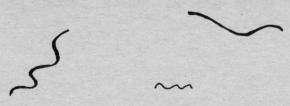

Chocolate Worms

Be ready for your guests' snack attacks with this super-gakky snacky.

You will need:
 1 small bag of chocolate chips
 1 small bag of butterscotch chips
 1 can of crunchy Chinese noodles
 wax paper
 1 adult to do the heating up

Here's what you do: Get an adult to melt the chocolate and butterscotch chips together in a saucepan. Then have the adult pour the melted sauce into a bowl. (Adults can be very useful sometimes.) Dump the noodles into the bowl and stir carefully. Now, using a long spoon, drop spoonfuls of the candy-covered noodles onto wax paper. Allow the worms to cool before eating.

Now that your guests are warmed up and well fed . . .

DOUBLE DARE Fast Fact: All the "soda pop" in the soda fountain obstacle is colored water.

Here Come the Obstacles!

Nothing makes a DOUBLE DARE overnight more exciting than a run through a wild and crazy obstacle course. Since DOUBLE DARE is dedicated to double-good fun, there are two obstacle courses—one to try at night, and the other for the morning after! So make sure your friends come prepared—with clothes they don't mind getting gakky.

The first one is fun, but not so sloppy—you can play it inside during your DOUBLE DARE overnight.

The second one is very sloppy—so save your skin, and the house, by trying it outside, in daylight, and with a parent's permission. The best time for a run through the DOUBLE DARE sloppy obstacle is right after breakfast. That way, just when your friends think that the overnight fun is over and it's time to go home, you can tell them the fun is *really* just beginning. After trekking through the Sloppy Obstacle Course, your friends will be so gakky you'll *want* to send them home!

The challenge is the same for both obstacle courses—a team of two must make it through!

NOTE: On DOUBLE DARE, you must make it through the obstacle course in 60 seconds—but in the game-book version just making it through is enough of a challenge. The time limit is up to you.

Here are some helpful hints on setting up your own DOUBLE DARE obstacle course.

1. Make sure you have plenty of room. The obstacles don't have to be very far apart, but remember, there are eight of them.

2. Be sure to set up the Sloppy Obstacle Course outside—some of these things are really gakky!

3. Be sure to have all your obstacles set up beforehand. That way you won't have to stop the fun to do it. One thing, though: be sure to leave the ice cream in the freezer until the very last minute—melted ice cream is too sloppy—even for a DOUBLE DARE Obstacle Course!

4. Line up in teams of two. One team at a time will go through the course. Remember, just like on DOUBLE DARE, the team members must take turns going through the obstacles. Be sure to read the instructions to the right player at each obstacle.

5. Wear old clothes!

The Not-So-Sloppy Obstacle Course

The course is designed to be done by a two-person team. You can be the host and read the instructions to each team. On your mark... get set... go!

Obstacle One:
You've Made Your Bed,
but Don't Lie in It!

You will need:
- 1 bed sheet
- 1 pillowcase
- 1 pillow
- 1 blanket
- 1 blindfold

The play: This is simple, it's something you do every day. All you have to do is make your bed. Of course, you do have to do it blindfolded. Put on the blindfold. Then put the sheet down on the floor. Cover it with the blanket. Put the case on the pillow, and put the pillow on top of the bed. But don't take that nap just yet. When you are through, take off the blindfold and hand it to your partner who must head over to...

DOUBLE DARE Fast Fact: On the average, one out of every four teams makes it all the way through the obstacle course.

Obstacle Two:
The Last Straw

You will need:
> 10 plastic drinking straws, the kind that
> come in paper wrappers

The play: All the straws are on the floor. Pick up
one straw. Peel the paper halfway off the straw.
Blow the remaining paper across the room. Once
you've blown three pieces of straw paper at least
five feet, hand a straw to your partner, who must
move like the wind to . . .

Obstacle Three:
Just Clowning Around

You will need:
> a small ball of Silly Putty or clay
> lipstick (ask permission to borrow Mom's)
> an oversized shirt (ask your dad or mom for
> an old one)
> a large pair of shoes (maybe your dad can
> loan you these, too.)

The play: Everybody loves a clown, and you are
about to be the most-loved clown of all—a
DOUBLE DARE clown. Put on the shirt and the
shoes. Draw big red lips, and top it all off with a
round nose made from putty or clay. When you
are done clowning around, hand your nose to
your partner, who should run over to . . .

Obstacle Four: Bundle Up!

You will need:

> a pair of mittens
> a shirt or jacket with buttons (big buttons preferred)
> a winter hat
> a winter scarf

The play: All you have to do is get bundled up in these winter clothes. There is one catch, though. You have to put on the mittens first! After you are all dressed, take off one mitten and hand it to your partner, who should run right over to . . .

Obstacle Five:
The Middle Man

You will need:

> A cookie jar or cookie box
> 15 cookies, including three sandwich cookies (the kind with creamy middles)

The play: You must reach into the cookie jar and pull out the three sandwich cookies. Separate the cookie halves and eat the creamy middle from each one. Then tag your partner, who will run over to the next obstacle.

Obstacle Six:
You Must Have Been a
Beautiful Baby!

You will need:
> 4 baby pictures
> 4 current pictures of the same people in the baby pictures

The play: A picture is worth a thousand words, and a good eye is worth valuable seconds. You must match the baby picture to the picture of the person today. Once you've got everyone matched up, hand one snapshot to your partner, who will shoot over to . . .

DOUBLE DARE Fast Fact: Dreaming up new obstacles is one of the best parts of working on DOUBLE DARE. When the producers and writers were coming up with new obstacles for SUPER-SLOPPY DOUBLE DARE, the first things they thought about were parts of the body. "Kids think parts of the body are funny," said Mike Klinghoffer. "And so do we." That's why there's now a giant foot obstacle, a mouth, a nose, and a giant head.

Obstacle Seven:
Best Foot Forward

You will need:
> 1 pair of really big adult shoes or boots (get permission first)
> 1 six-foot long piece of masking tape stuck to the floor in a straight line. (It has to be masking tape. Any other tape could damage the floor.)

The play: All you do is put on the shoes and walk the line. But just to make it more interesting, you have to put the left shoe on your right foot and the right shoe on your left foot. Then put one foot in front of the other and walk the length of the masking-tape line. If you lose your balance you have to go back to start. Both feet must be on the line at all times. When you're done, take off the shoes and tag your partner, who will hotfoot it over to . . .

DOUBLE DARE Fast Fact: DOUBLE DARE is designed so that no one ever has to give a wrong answer. Think about it. If you don't know something, you can always take the physical challenge.

Obstacle Eight:
I Scream, You Make the Cone!

You will need:
- 1 ice-cream cone
- 1 container of ice cream
- 1 ice-cream scooper
- chopped nuts
- 1 cherry
- 1 blindfold
- 1 newspaper

The play: All the ingredients are lined up on the newspaper. Your job is to make a super-scrumptious ice-cream cone, using all the ingredients. So why the newspaper? It's there to make sure you don't get gakky, since you will be doing this blindfolded. Once your cone is topped off with the cherry, take off the blindfold and dig in. After the licking you've both taken, licking an ice-cream cone is the perfect DOUBLE DARE reward!

Now that you're all obstacled out, it's probably time to hit the sack. Of course you're all going to go straight to sleep the way you always do at overnights . . . right? Well, you better try to get some sleep, because there's lots more DOUBLE DARE fun to come!

There's Got to Be a Morning After

Rise and shine! It's a new day and there's lots of DOUBLE DARE action waiting for you. But first you'd better build up your strength. These yummy, gooey, out-of-this-world pancake recipes will be just what Dr. DOUBLE DARE ordered!

Let an adult make the actual pancakes. You save your strength for putting on the toppings and putting it all away!

Sunday Slide Pancakes

You will need:
    a stack of 3 pancakes
    1 scoop vanilla ice cream
    butterscotch sauce
    whipped cream

Here's what you do: Top the pancakes with the ice cream and butterscotch sauce. Cover the whole thing with whipped cream.

DOUBLE DARE Pear Pancakes

You will need:

    a stack of 3 pancakes
    1 scoop butter pecan ice cream
    ½ canned Bartlett pear
    chocolate sauce

Here's what you do: Cover the pancakes with the ice cream. Stack the pear on top of the ice cream and top with lots of ooey, gooey chocolate sauce.

Going Bananas Pancakes

You will need:

    butter or margarine
    a stack of 3 pancakes
    peanut butter
    a sliced large banana

Here's what you do: Butter each pancake. Spread peanut butter on each pancake. Top each with bananas. Restack the pancakes.

Now you should be happy and ready for . . .
The Sloppy Obstacle Course

Remember: Only try this outdoors and with a parent's permission!

The Sloppy Obstacle Course

Obstacle One:
Strawberry Snort Cake

You will need:

1 bowl of whipped cream

2 strawberries

The play: The strawberries are hidden in the whipped cream. It's up to you to find one of them and eat it. But there is one catch—you can't use your hands! That's right, it's sort of like bobbing for apples. Once you've eaten the strawberry, tag your partner, who'll whip on over to . . .

Obstacle Two:
You Must be Yolking!

You will need:

1 egg

2 bowls

The play: This obstacle is exactly what we mean when we say GAK! You must crack the egg into a bowl and separate the yolk from the white— using only your hands! Dump the yolk in the second bowl, then shake hands with your partner (GAK!). Your partner then eggs-its to . . .

Obstacle Three:
A Model Player!

You will need:
 1 blindfold
 1 plastic bowl of water

The play: This is a DOUBLE DARE modeling lesson. Put on the blindfold. Then put the bowl of water on your head. Walk five feet to the finish line. If you get there and all the water has spilled out, you've got to go back and start again. But if you reach the line with some water in the bowl, pour the last bit of water over your partner's head. Then watch as your partner skedaddles over to . . .

Obstacle Four:
No Small Feet!

You will need:
 whipped cream
 1 cupcake

The play: This one's a piece of cake. All you have to do is spread some whipped cream all over the cupcake. There's just one small catch—you have to use your feet! So take off your shoes, dip your toes in the whipped cream, and start spreading the sweet stuff. When you're through, tag your partner. Then you can clean your twinkling toes and put your shoes back on while your partner tries . . .

Obstacle Five:
Going Crackers

You will need:
>4 crackers (the drier the better)
>1 piece of paper with the secret message written on it

The play: Put all four crackers in your mouth— chew but don't swallow. Now read the secret message out loud. Nothing to it. Here's the secret message:

>The Sixth Sheik's Sixth Son is Sick
>Peter Piper Picked a Peck of Pretty Putrid Peppers
>Theophilus Thistle the Successful Thistle Sifter, Sifted Six Thistles this Sunday

Once you've read the message, tag your partner, who should head on over to . . .

〰〰〰〰〰〰〰〰〰〰〰〰

DOUBLE DARE Fast Fact: All the drippy, messy food that is used on DOUBLE DARE is what they call "stale-dated" food. It's food that would otherwise be thrown out. DOUBLE DARE uses stale-dated food because the producers don't want to waste good food.

〰〰〰〰〰〰〰〰〰〰〰〰

Obstacle Six:
You're a Shooting Star!

You will need:

    3 filled water guns
    1 three-sheet streamer of paper toweling
    2 sticks

The play: Don't shoot until you see the whites of
the paper towel! In this case, the paper towels
are taped to two sticks and stretched out like a
banner. Two people hold the sticks so the banner
is stretched out straight. Standing three feet
from the banner, shoot water at the paper banner
until it soaks through and tears. As soon as the
banner is split, hand the gun to your pardner. . .
uh. . . er. . . partner, who must split for. . .

 # Obstacle Seven:
You Can Dish it Out!

You will need:

    5 paper plates
    1 bucket of water

The play: We're sorry, but we interrupt this
obstacle course so you can do the dishes. The
paper plates are stacked neatly. Throw each one
like a Frisbee to your partner. Your partner must
catch the plate, soak it in the bucket, and stack
it. When all the dishes are stacked, run with your
partner over to. . .

Obstacle Eight:
Can You Stomach This?

You will need:

1 chair (Make sure you have permission. The chair may get gakky.)

1 table covered with an anti-gak plastic cloth

1 ice-cream scooper

1 container of ice cream

1 dish of chocolate syrup

1 spray can of whipped cream

1 cherry

3 spoons

1 bowl

The play: The sundae ingredients are placed on a table next to the chair. Your partner lies on the floor and holds the bowl on his or her stomach. You sit on the chair right behind your partner. Now start your sundae. Get a nice, big scoop of ice cream. Then take aim, and plop the scoop into the bowl on your partner's belly. Then get a big spoonful of chocolate sauce. Let it dribble off the spoon and into the bowl. Follow it up by shooting a cool stream of whipped cream over the sauce. Finally, top it off with a DOUBLE DARE yummy cherry bomb! When you've got everything in the bowl, you and your partner can belly up to the table for the spoons, and dig in!